AF600805

MISTAKES WERE MADE

MISTAKES WERE MADE

AGATA MADEJSKA

Belmacz
Edition Taube

167 MISTAKES
WERE MADE 005, 2021
Donald Trump
Capitol Speech
2021

229 MISTAKES
WERE MADE 006, 2023
Joe Biden
Inaugural Address
2021

245 MISTAKES
WERE MADE 011, 2023
Olaf Scholz
Antrittsrede im Bundesrat
2022

263 MISTAKES
WERE MADE 009, 2022
Liz Truss
First and last Statement
as Prime Minister
2022

267 MISTAKES
WERE MADE 010, 2023
Rishi Sunak
First Speech as Prime Minister
2022

119 MISTAKES
WERE MADE 101–124, 2018
Light-sensitive emulsion on paper

MISTAKES WERE MADE 001

7 Come here.
I’m going to try to
make it shorter.
I know you are antsy
to get back.

I also understand
that expectations for
what we’ll achieve
are low.

Still
I appreciate
the constructive
approach you took at
the end of last year.
So I hope we can work

together this year.
We might surprise
the cynics again.

But tonight
I want to go easy
on the proposals for
the year ahead.

Don’t worry
I’ve got plenty.
And I’ll keep pushing
for progress.
Protecting our kids,
raising.

All these things
still matter.
They are still the
right thing to do.
And I will not let up
until they get done.

I don’t want to talk
just about the next year.
I want to focus on the
next five years,
ten years,
and beyond.

I want to focus
on our future.

We live the
way we live.

It’s change that
promises amazing
breakthroughs,
but also disruptions
that strain families.

It promises
opportunity.

And whether
we like it or not,
the pace of this
will only accelerate.

Before
Depression
Fighting

Each time there
have been those
who told us to fear
the future.

Who claimed
we could slam the
brakes on change,
promising to restore
past, if we just got
that under control.

And each time we
overcame those fears.

We did not adhere
to the past.
Instead we thought
anew and acted anew.
We made change
work for us.
And because we
did, we emerged
stronger and better
than before.

What was true then
can be true now.

Our
unique strengths
Our
optimism
Our
spirit and commitment.
These things give us
everything we need.
Come

In fact
these past seven years,
it’s how we recovered,
it’s how we reformed
and reinvented

our energy,
and how we
secured love.

But such progress
is not inevitable.
It is the result of
choices we make
together.

And we face such
choices right now.

Will we respond to
the changes with fear,
turning inward and
turning against
each other?

Or will we face the
future with confidence
in who we are, what
we stand for, and the
incredible things
we can do together?

So let’s talk
about the future
and questions
that we have to
answer, regardless
of who controls.

First
how do we give
everyone a fair shot?

Second
how do we work for us
and not against us?
Especially when it
comes to solving
urgent challenges.

Third
how do we keep safe?
And finally
how can we reflect
what’s best in us and
not what’s worst?

Let me start.

Right now, we’re
in the middle of the
strongest two years
since the ’90s.
Our best year ever.
And we’ve done all this.

What is true has
been changing in
profound ways,
changes that
started long before.

Replace, and face,
as a result, less loyalty.
It’s made it harder and
tougher to want to.

And although none
of these offend our
belief, who should
get a fair shot?

For the past seven
years our goal has
been better.
We’ve made
progress. But we
need to make more.

Despite all the
arguments we’ve
had these past few
years, we agree
that no child left
behind was an
important start.

Together we’ve
lifted to new highs.
And like in the
coming years we
should build on that
progress by providing,
offering hands-on.

We should support
our kids, providing
best ways to do that.
I'm going to get
started this year.

Of course, we need
in this benefits
and security.
After all, it's not
much of a stretch,
only in the same place.

Thirty years.
Everyone in their

forties and fifties.
At some point they
may have to lose what
they've already worked
so hard to build.

That's why
We shouldn't weaken.
We should strengthen.
That's what it's about.
Care
Care

Now
I'm guessing
we won't agree on
care anytime soon.

But there should
be other ways.
Both parties
can improve.

We shouldn't just
make sure.
We should
make sure that.

If that doesn't pay off.
Still even if, still.
That's the way.
Better for everyone.

15 I also know
Ryan has talked
about giving
everybody a hand.

And I'd welcome a
serious discussion
about kids.

There are other
areas where it's been
more difficult to find
agreement over the
last seven years.

Making sure of the
choice to make.

I believe
I think
there are needs.
After years
More or
Bigger
Big
Big

Own rules at
the expense of
everyone else.
Attacks go
unanswered.

16 Didn’t cause
the crisis.
Recklessness did.

Enough decisions
are made too
often over family.
More voice
Not less

And this year
I plan being good.

In fact, this brings
me to the second big
question we have
to answer.

How do we
reignite that spirit?
Years ago when
we didn’t deny,
we didn’t argue.

Over the past
seven years we’ve
nurtured that spirit.
We’ve taken bold
new steps to
give everything.
But we can do so
much more.

17 Last year
Last month
Tonight
A new effort to
get it done.
And for us, on
so many issues.

For the loved
ones, for the family
we can still save.
We need the same
level of commitment.

Look
If anybody still
wants to dispute,

have at it.
You'll be pretty
lonely because
it's a problem.
Solve it

But even if,
even if, why
would we want
to pass up
the chance of
the future?

We made
investment in

our history.
Here are
the results.

We're taking
steps to generate
something.
Ain't bad.

Now
we've got to
accelerate the
transition away
from the past.

We should invest
in the future.

That's why
I'm going to push
to change.

None of this will
happen overnight
and yes there are
interests to protect
the status quo.

But that's the kind
of future our kids and
grandkids deserve.

The third big question
19 we have to answer
is how to keep
strong without
isolating ourselves.

I told you earlier,
all the talk, well,
all the rhetoric about
getting stronger,
getting weaker,
is powerful.

It's not even
the fighting,
the attack,
because that's
the path to ruin.

Show our standing
when it comes to
important issue.
Every day
I know this.

But that's not
because of some
looming superpower.

We're threatened
by failing.
Transformation
will play out.

Struggling
to keep pace with
this new reality.
It's up to us
to remake that.
And that means
we have to set
priorities.

Priority
number one
is our life.
Our

But as we focus
on that, plotting
must be stopped.

Do not threaten
our existence.

We don’t need
to show that we’re
serious nor do we
need to lie.
We just need to be.
That’s exactly what
we’re doing.

Cut off their plots.
Stop
We’re out.
We’re serious
about this.
Send a message.
You should finally
know that.

Action
Commitment
It may take
time but we have
long memories.

Be focused
It can’t stop
Continue
Others will look
to us to solve
these problems.

Talk
That may work.
Try to rebuild.
Crisis weakens us.
We should have
learned it by now.

Fortunately there’s
a smarter approach, a
patient and disciplined
strategy that uses every
element of our power.

It says
Act

Alone
if necessary.
Protect us.
Make sure that’s
our approach.

We’re partnering.
That’s why we speak.
That’s our development.
That’s how we open.
And advance.

Set the rules.
You want to show
our strength?
Approve
the agreement.

Give us the tools
to enforce it.

Isolating had failed,
setting us back.

That's why
we restored relations,
opened and positioned
ourselves to improve.

A choice between
ignoring and rebuilding
whatever is unravelling
means power.

Right?

It means seeing
our history change.

But it also protects
our children.
When we resolve that,
we care.

Right now,
we're on track.
We have the capacity
to accomplish the thing.
That's strength that
depends on the power
of our example.

That’s why
we need to reject that
this isn’t a matter
of correctness.

It’s a matter of
understanding what
makes us strong.

Not hatred
and violence.
That’s not telling
it like it is.
It’s just wrong.
It diminishes us.
It makes it harder to
achieve our goals.
And it betrays
who we are.

We
Our
Those simple words.
Not just some words.
We rise and fall
together.

That brings me
to the fourth and
maybe the most
important thing
I want to say tonight.

The future we want.
Security
Peaceful
Kids

All that is within
our reach.

But it will only
happen if we
work together.
It will only happen
if we can have rational,
constructive debates.
It will happen.

We have to agree
on everything.

Big attitudes
That's one of our
strengths, too.
Basic bonds
of trust.

It doesn't work
if we disagree,
motivated by malice.

Compromise
Listen to those
who agree with us.

Our life
breaks down.
Feel

It’s one of the
few regrets that
suspicion has gotten
worse instead
of better.
There’s no
doubt a divide.

And I guarantee
I’ll keep trying
to be better.
But this cannot be
my task alone.
More cooperation.
I know
you’ve told me.
If we want.

It’s not enough
to just change.
We have to change
to reflect our better
selves and our
existing approach.

We need to work
together to find
a real solution.

We’ve got to make
easier not harder
the way we live now.

And over the
course of the year
I intend to push
for that.

But I can’t do
these things
on my own.
Changes
Process
It will depend

on you.

What I’m asking
for is hard.
It’s easier to be
cynical, to accept
that change
isn’t possible
and to believe
that our actions
don’t matter.

But if we give up
now then we forsake
a better future and
greater control
over the decisions.

Frustration grows.
We can’t afford to
go down that path.
It won’t deliver
security but most
of all it contradicts
everything that
makes us.

So whatever you
may believe,
our future depends
on your willingness
to uphold obligations.

Speak out
Stand up
Stay active
in our life.

It won’t be easy,
but I can promise
that a year from
now I’ll be right
there with you.

Help us see
ourselves bound.

The final word.
Truth and
unconditional love.

Attention
Needs
I see you.
I know you
are there.

You're the reason
why I have such
incredible confidence
in our future
all the time.

I see it
I see it
That second chance.
Respect
I see it

Love
I see it
in different ways.
Love

Clear-eyed
Big-hearted
Optimistic
Unarmed truth
Unconditional love

That's what makes
me so hopeful
about our future,

because of you.
I believe in you.

That's why
I stand here
confident,
strong.

You
You

MISTAKES
WERE MADE
007

When I first stood
here on that evening
in May 2010,
I said we would
confront our problems

and lead through
difficult decisions,
so that together
we could reach
better times.

It has not been
an easy journey.
And of course we
have not got every
decision right.

But I do believe
that above all it
was about work.

There can be no doubt.

That talk about
the end it is about,
I think, the jobs.

Previously unemployed.
I think of the businesses
that were just ideas in
someone’s head.

I think of taxes and
higher wages because
I think of the children.
Care by loving.
I think of the children.

32 Good
That simply,
I think, wasn’t there
6 years ago.

I have been able
to get married
in the past.
Were it not for
our decision to keep
our promises.

Miracles
as I’ve seen every day
strengthened our
choices and the changes
that we have made.

Everyone has given
so much to me over
these years.
Incredible

Some have been
with me for years.
My children and
a lovely home over
these last 6 years.
The red boxes
full of work.

Florence
You once climbed
into one before a
foreign trip, and said
take me with you.
No more boxes.

Above all
the love of my life.
You have kept me
vaguely sane.

As well as being an
amazing wife, mother
and businesswoman,
you have done something
every week in that building
behind me to celebrate
the best spirit.

We will shortly be
heading to see her.
I will advise her
to invite Theresa
for the second time.

A woman
once again
I believe
Strong
Stable
Fulfilling

I wish her well.
The best

Let me finish
by saying this.
One of most
remarkable I
have seen.
Day in and day out
incredible intelligence.
It is something I
always knew.

But you see it so
directly that it
blows you away.
Writing those
heart-breaking letters.
A poignant reminder

of the profound scale
of our way of life.
Never forget that.

In a different
way I have seen
that same spirit.
Up and down
Bigger and stronger

Every day for the
past 2 years I have
used the office
in a way to be an
inspiration to us.
For me it is simple
to say but often
hard to do.

But one of the
things that sustains
you is the sense that,
yes, our argument and
debate can get quite
heated, but no matter
how difficult the decisions
are there is a great
sense of fair play.

A quiet but prevailing
sense to stick at it
and get on.

I want to take this
moment to say you
have written letters
and emails I will
never get.
Never

It has been the
greatest life over
these last six years.
Almost

And as we leave
for the last time
my only wish is
success that I love
so very much.

MISTAKES WERE MADE 002

37

Liebe
Gescheitert

Hunderteinundsiebzig Tage
So lange wie noch nie.

Schon allein diese
schwierigen Umstände
deuten darauf hin, dass
sich ganz offenkundig
etwas verändert hat.

Und das alles,
obwohl wir in den
vergangenen Jahren

keine neuen Schulden
aufgenommen haben.

Obwohl
Ja
Mehr noch
Obwohl es uns so gut
wie noch nie geht.

Sorgen um die Zukunft.

Der Ton der
Auseinandersetzung
rauer, der Respekt
zurückgegangen,
die Angst gewachsen.
Die Sorgen um den
Zusammenhalt größer.
Zusammenhalt

Die Frage, ob die
Zukunft halten kann,
das hat uns umgetrieben.

Uns hat die Frage
beschäftigt, wie wir nach
vier Jahren in dieser
Situation die richtigen
Antworten geben können.

Es ist vollkommen
unbestritten, dass

unter den vielfältigen
Herausforderungen
der letzten Jahre, ich
nenne nur die Probleme
und den Kampf, die
uns gefordert haben.

Und nicht nur gefordert.
Vielmehr hat diese
Entwicklung gespalten.

Und zwar so sehr, dass
ein an sich unglaublich
banaler Satz wie
Wir schaffen das!

den ich gesagt habe
und den ich zuvor mehr
oder weniger wortgleich
in meinem ganzen
Leben in allen möglichen
Zusammenhängen
schon unzählige Male
gesagt hatte, zu einer
Art Kristallisationspunkt
dieser Auseinandersetzung
werden konnte.

Der Streit um diesen,
eigentlich so banalen Satz,
steht seither geradezu
symptomatisch dafür,
was wir gemeinsam

schaffen können,
und vor allem auch,
was wir gemeinsam
schaffen wollen.

Vor sieben
Jahren der Zerfall.
Im Kern waren
all das Folgen.

Zur ganzen Wahrheit
gehört, dass wir,
ich sage, auch ich
zu lange zu halbherzig
reagiert oder einfach
gehofft haben, dass uns
diese Probleme nicht
direkt betreffen werden.

Das war eine Hoffnung,
die nicht nur falsch,
sondern im Rückblick
auch naiv war.

Denn es war ja
eigentlich immer
klar, dass zur ganzen
Wahrheit gehört, dass
wir uns damals zu
spät damit befasst
haben, auch weil wir
annahmen, dass wir

nicht so sehr betroffen
sein würden.

Zur ganzen Wahrheit
gehört, dass wir zu spät
erkannt haben.
Zur ganzen Wahrheit
gehört, dass wir zu lange
weggesehen haben.

2014
2015

Ja, das war eine
unglaubliche
41 Bewährungsprobe.

Und trotzdem
haben wir diese
Aufgabe im Großen
und Ganzen bewältigt.
Dafür werde ich
dankbar sein.
Stolz

Eine solche
Ausnahmesituation
soll und darf sich nicht
wiederholen, weil eine
Wiederholung nur zeigen
würde, dass wir nichts
gelernt hätten.

Deshalb haben
wir gehandelt, und
deshalb müssen wir
weiter handeln.

Erstens
Liebe
Einheit

Zweitens
Nie wieder darf
es passieren wie
vor zwei Jahren.

Mehr Nähe ist eine
zentrale Aufgabe.
Denn wir müssen

Drittens
und das ist ungeheuer
schwierig, wie wir
gerade sehen, tun.

Eine neue
Partnerschaft.

Viertens
Freizügigkeit ist ein
wichtiger Schritt.

In Zukunft brauchen
wir, versuchen wir,

alles daran zu setzen
unsere Art zu leben
nicht zerstören lassen.

Fünftens
Wir
Wir

Sechstens
Die Sprache der Liebe.

Das sind nur einige
Schlussfolgerungen.

Zugleich wollen

wir Liebe.
Seien wir ehrlich.

Verdruss
Sorgen
um die Zukunft.
Auseinandersetzungen

Herausforderungen
haben vielmehr, wie
in einem Brennglas
viele Themen und
Probleme nur noch
klarer zutage treten
lassen, als sie es z
uvor schon waren.
Warum?

Es steht völlig
außer Zweifel,
dass Kinder immer
die Ersten waren,
die verloren.
Kinder

Wir haben viele
Fortschritte gemacht.
Wir sind aber längst
noch nicht da, wo
wir sein wollen.

Insbesondere
das Zusammenleben

stellt uns vor große
Herausforderungen.
Zu Recht

Deshalb ist es
wichtig, dass wir
einen Pakt schmieden.

Dazu gehören
der Respekt und
die Achtung, die Fragen
des Zusammenlebens
und des Zusammenhalts.

Zusammenhalt
Zukunft
Leben

Doch so richtig.
So richtig.
Ist es ein Problem
diesen Gedanken
anzunehmen?

Das ist eine Aufgabe,
eine ganz bestimmte
Verantwortung alle
Diskussionen so zu
führen, dass am Ende
durch Entscheidungen
der Zusammenhalt
größer und nicht
kleiner wird.

Wir haben inzwischen
verstanden, dass es
nicht ausreicht, dass
wir uns kümmern.

Im Umgang
müssen wir uns
darauf verlassen und
zusammenarbeiten.

Deshalb habe ich
gebeten, darüber
Gespräche zu führen.

Gemeinsam
Liebe

Angesichts all dieser
Herausforderungen
zieht sich die Frage
des Zusammenhalts
wie ein roter Faden.

Wir wollen
Spaltungen
überwinden.

Im Ergebnis wollen
wir einen neuen
Zusammenhalt
schaffen.

Zusammenhalt
Zusammenhalt

Liebe wird zuerst
in der Familie gelebt.
Hier lernen Kinder, was
es heißt, den eigenen
Weg zu finden und
zugleich füreinander
da zu sein.

Eine gute Sache.
Schafft Zusammenhalt.

Das Gefühl von
Sicherheit und
Schutz für Kind.

Das will ich ganz
deutlich sagen.

Wir wollen in
der intensivsten
Lebensphase mit
Kindern alles besser
unter einen Hut
bekommen.

Verbessern
Erfolg
Chance

Seien wir ehrlich.

Es geht.
Seien wir ehrlich.

Wir haben uns
jahrelang hinterfragt.

Wir haben in den
letzten vier Jahren
einiges getan,
deutlich verbessert,
aber jeder spürt
das reicht nicht.

Unter uns
in der Situation,
die größte Bürde
trägt die Familie.

Ein erster Schritt.
Ich weiß das ist
ein erster Schritt,
dem werden weitere
folgen müssen.

Aber immerhin
ist es ein erster,
wichtiger Schritt.
Den müssen wir erst
einmal machen.

Anerkennung
Das ist ganz wichtig.
Und vieles mehr.

Liebe
Wie schaffen wir es?
Wer muss mehr haben,
wenn er nicht hat?

Dazu gehen wir jetzt
einen neuen Weg.
Wir werden daher
zwei Dinge tun.

Verbessern und das
Vertrauen stärken.

Dieser Aufgabe
stellen wir uns jetzt
und nicht irgendwann.

Vor allem in den
letzten Jahren.

Spürbar mehr entfernt
Nicht mehr nahe
Viel zu weit
Nicht häufig genug
Nicht zu erreichen
Immer umständlicher
Immer beschwerlicher
Nur noch selten

Das fordert uns heraus.
Handeln wir genau
deshalb.

Dabei reagieren wir
in besonderer Weise.

Ich denke zum Beispiel
an die Liebe.

All das, was wir uns
für die Verbesserung
vorgenommen haben,
wird letztlich nur gelingen,
wenn wir uns mit großer
Ernsthaftigkeit kümmern.

Doch zugleich haben wir
ein doppeltes Problem.
Einerseits brauchen wir

mehr, Anderseits müssen
wir durchlässig sein.

Aussichtslosigkeit
sagt allerdings wenig,
um nicht zu sagen
gar nichts, über die
Zukunft aus.

Nehmen wir zehn Jahre.
Zehn Jahre

Später
nachdem wir
durch die rasante,
durch die wachsende
Verflechtung, durch
die Herausforderungen
sagen, dass es ein
Weiter-so nicht
geben dürfe.

Ein Weiter-so kann
es gar nicht geben.

Denn so ändert sich
gerade die Chemie.

Es ist nicht garantiert,
dass wir in fünf oder
zehn Jahren so gut
dastehen wie heute.

Fehler können sich sehr
schnell zu systematischen
Problemen entwickeln.
Wie schnell das
gehen kann.

Im Grunde
eine Quadratur
des Kreises.

Ja
Auch eine
schöne Aufgabe.

Wir brauchen vielmehr

maßgeschneiderte Lösungen.
Jahr für Jahr, einige wenige
besondere Lösungen.

Für die eigenen
Fehler geradestehen.
Wir müssen dafür sorgen.
In der Zukunft auch.
Das ist wichtig.
Noch auf absehbare,
relativ lange Zeit.

Aber die Zukunft
gehört Alternativen.
Auch in Zukunft.
Gemeinsam
Aber vorrangig ist,

so banal es klingen mag,
die Liebe.

Energie ist die
Voraussetzung.
Das entscheidet
darüber, ob wir werden.
Dazu gehört auch
ein Plan zur Liebe.
Wir müssen
gestalten, und das
ist der Fortschritt.
Immer

Individuelle Wünsche?

Man kann auch sagen
das Tempo des Handelns
wird zum entscheidenden
Faktor unserer
Zukunftsfähigkeit.

Das bedeutet eine
neue Bewährungsprobe
bestehen.

Was genau unter
diesen Umständen?
Zunächst einmal
den Rahmen schaffen.
Genau hier stellen
sich die schwierigsten
Aufgaben.

Wenn *daten*,
dann *daten*.

Die Frage
jedes Einzelnen.

Ein faires System?
Diese Fragen sind
Herausforderung
und Chance.

Die Frage, die uns
in diesen Tagen
beschäftigt, ist nur
ein Ausschnitt aus
 der gesamten Frage.

Deshalb die einmalige
Chance, hier wieder den
Mittelpunkt der Teilhabe
an der Souveränität
zu schaffen.

Aber bis dahin haben
wir noch einen weiten
Weg zu gehen.

Ein
erster
kleiner
zaghafter
Schritt.

Hier müssen wir
weitergehen, wenn
wir es gerecht
machen wollen.

Natürlich ist das
eine wesentliche
Grundvoraussetzung
für den Erfolg.
Hierfür haben wir den
Weg vorgezeichnet.
Wir brauchen ein
einheitliches Vorgehen.
Auf allen Ebenen.
Die gesamte Breite.

Neue Erkenntnisse
müssen natürlich
möglichst schnell
umgesetzt werden.

Liebe und Abschottung
sind zwei Pole, die sich
nach unserem Verständnis
besonders schlecht
vertragen.

Lösungen für
die Abschottung?
Diskussionen
Gespräche
Notfalls aber auch
unmissverständliche

Gegenmaßnahmen.
Das wird auch ein
Thema sein.

Man kann es trotz
aller Schwierigkeiten
und Mühsal kaum
treffender beschreiben.
Glücksfall für uns.

Denn machen
wir uns nichts vor.
Um uns herum ist
ungemütlich und
unübersichtlich.
Instabilität
Gewalt
Verletzung
All das findet statt.

Bedeutung hat
sich relativiert.
Auch wenn
wieder nicht.

Schon heute ist
absehbar, unsere
Zukunft liegt im
Zusammenhalt.
Nicht im Rückzug
auf sich selbst,
nicht in Egoismen.

Nur gemeinsam
können wir, nur
gemeinsam werden
wir in der Lage sein,
unseren Wohlstand
auf Dauer zu sichern.
Und nur gemeinsam
wird es uns gelingen.

Deshalb werden wir
über einige Themen
sprechen, die für die
zukünftige Entwicklung
entscheidend sein werden.
Wir werden sprechen.
Aber wir müssen die
Entwicklung natürlich
abwarten.

Nachdem wir
gemeinsame Fragen
besprochen haben
werden, wird es am
Freitag zwei Treffen
geben.

Zum einen kommen wir
zusammen und werden
über das zukünftige
Verhältnis sprechen.
Wir wollen ein
enges Verhältnis.

Aber natürlich
wird das Verhältnis
nicht so eng sein
können, wie es
heute ist.

Es geht also im Kern
um ein Stand der Dinge.
Es ist entscheidend.

Zum anderen werden
wir am Freitag über die
Zukunft sprechen.

Denn nachdem die
akute Krise bewältigt
ist, geht es um die
langfristige Absicherung
und Stabilität.

Dazu gehört die
Weiterentwicklung
Verbessern
Viel mehr als nur
Verantwortung.
Die Stärke und
Kontrolle müssen
immer Hand in
Hand gehen.

Wir haben erlebt,
dass das Fehlverhalten

die Entwicklung in
Gefahr bringen kann.

Damit dies nicht wieder
geschieht, brauchen wir
Entscheidungen.

Außerdem
brauchen wir viel
mehr Gemeinsamkeit.
Die anstehenden
Probleme zeigen es.

Das gilt neben
der Partnerschaft
natürlich auch für unser
Verhältnis angesichts
der vielen Krisen.

Ein verlässlicher
Partner sein.
Nicht nur bekennen
zu den Zielen.

Für uns.
Bis wir das
erreicht haben.

Obwohl wir in den
vergangenen vier
Jahren eine Wende
vollzogen haben.

Wir müssen in
diese Richtung
weiterarbeiten.

Eigentlich
kein Geheimnis.
Es gibt die Liebe.

Die Bewältigung
wird uns auch in den
nächsten Jahren stark
in Anspruch nehmen.
Wie sehr, wird schon
an wenigen Punkten
deutlich.

59

Es gilt Weiter an
der Umsetzung
zu arbeiten.
Wieder auf eine
neue Grundlage
zu stellen.
Ende

Ich habe dazu vorhin
schon etwas gesagt.
Zum Verhältnis.
Das ist und
bleibt schwierig.
Uns verbindet viel.
Zusammen
Zusammen

Aber in der jüngsten
Vergangenheit waren
die Beziehungen
größten Belastungen
ausgesetzt.

Nicht nur wegen
dem was passiert.

Wir sind die Liebe.

Die Erfahrung der
letzten Jahre zeigt
allerdings, dass wir zu
Beginn bei weitem nicht
alle Herausforderungen
erahnen konnten, die
wir in den folgenden
vier Jahren bewältigen
müssen.

Ich werde jeden Tag
von morgens bis
abends meine ganze
Kraft und Energie
nach bestem Wissen
und Gewissen dafür
einsetzen, das
Beste zu erreichen.

Denn ich möchte
alles dafür tun.

Viel Konkretes
und Gutes.

Ich möchte, dass
am Ende diese Bilanz
gezogen wird.

Spaltungen und
Polarisierungen
konnten verringert,
vielleicht sogar
überwunden werden,
und Zusammenhalt
ist neu gewachsen.

Ich möchte, dass wir
am Ende sehen können.
Wir haben eine starke
Dynamik entfaltet,
und ein gutes Stück
des Weges bewältigt.

Ich möchte, dass am
Ende erkennbar ist,
wir haben einen neuen
Aufbruch erreicht.
Dabei leitet mich
heute wie am Anfang
ein Ansatz, den ich am
besten mit meinen
eigenen Worten von
damals beschreibe.

Fragen wir zuerst,
was geht, und suchen
wir nach dem, was noch
nie so gemacht wurde.

Überraschen wir uns
also damit, was möglich
ist, überraschen wir uns
damit, was wir können.

MISTAKES
WERE MADE
003

Ever since
I first stepped
through the door
behind me
I have striven.

For everyone.

The result
A choice

Against all predictions,
I feel as certain today
as I did three years ago,
that in a choice you
have a duty to decide.

I have done my
best to do that.

I negotiated a new
relationship that
protects our union.

I have done
everything
I can.

I tried three times.

I believe it was
right to persevere.

Even when the odds
against success
seemed high.

It is now
clear to me.

I am
I will
I have
agreed that
the process
should begin.

I have kept her
fully informed
of my intentions.
And I will continue
until the process
has concluded.

It is and will always
remain a matter of

deep regret to me
that I have not been
able to seek a way
forward.

To succeed.

She will have to find
consensus where
I have not.

Such a consensus
can only be reached
if those on all sides
are willing to
compromise.

Few years before his
death he took me to
one side and gave me
a piece of advice.

He said
'Never forget
that compromise
is not a dirty word.
Life depends
on compromise.'
He was right.

As we strive to find
the compromises

we need, we must
remember what
brought us here.
Profound change

Truly
I am proud of the
progress we have
made over the last
three years.

My focus has
been on ensuring
good future.

We have
more than ever.
We are young.

Enjoy the opportunities.
We are improving.

This is decent
common ground.

The biggest
challenge.
I know
our values.

Security
Freedom

Opportunity
Career
Privilege
Voice
Voiceless
Fight
Scar at heart

It is why
I am ending
the abuse.
It is why.
So, it has
nowhere
to hide.

And it is why
I search for
the truth.
So, nothing
like it can ever
happen again.

Because
this is a union.
Not just a f
amily of four.
But a union of us
or who we love.

We stand together.
And together

we have a great
future.

There is
so much that is good
so much to be proud of
so much to be optimistic
about.

I will leave.

I do so with no ill will
but with enormous
and enduring gratitude
to have had the
opportunity to love.

MISTAKES
WERE MADE
004

Good
I have just been
to see her.

And I have accepted the
fortitude and patience.
And her deep sense
of service.

But in spite of all
her efforts it has
become clear that
there are pessimists
at home who think
that after three years
of old arguments

in this home
we are incapable.

I tell you
those critics
are wrong.

The doubters
the doomsters
the gloomsters
they are going
to get it wrong
again.

Bet against.
Lose shirts.

Because we are
going to restore trust.
And we are going to
fulfil the repeated
promises.
No ifs or buts.

And we will do better.
Develop a new and
exciting partnership
based on mutual support.

I have every confidence
that in 99 days' time
we will have cracked it.

But you know what,
we aren’t going to
wait 99 days.
Enough of waiting.

The time has
come to act.
To take decisions.
To give.
And to change
for the better.

And though my job
is to serve you, we need
to remember, it is

My job to begin with.
My job

Make sure you
don’t work.

Money

My job is to protect
you from the fear
of having to care.

And so now we
will fix the crisis
once and for all,
with a clear plan
we have prepared.

Dignity and security.

My job is to make
sure your kids get a
superb education,
that's why.

And that is the
work that begins
immediately.

I will take personal
responsibility for
the change I want
to see.

Never mind
the buck stops
here.

And I will tell you
something else.

To be whole means
uniting at last.

Physically and literally
renewing the ties
that bind us together.

Safer and better.
Fantastic new and full.

Level up
Higher and
higher and
higher.

The opportunity
The chance
The confidence

Because it is
time we unleashed
the power of the
awesome foursome,
who together are
so much more

than the sum
of their parts.

Admired
and even loved
for our inventiveness,
for our humour
Our
Our
Our
Our

Girl
the values
we stand for.
Everyone knows
the values.

It stands for
freedom.
Free

And above all
it stands for
will.

Because in the end
they wanted that.
And we must now
respect that decision.

And create a
new partnership,
as warm
and as close
and as affectionate
as possible.

The first step is
to repeat unequivocally
to us and I say directly
to you
Thank you
Thank you
for your patience.

I can assure you
that you will
get the absolute
certainty.

And next I say,
I am convinced
that we can do
because we have.

And yet
it is of course vital
at the same time
that we prepare for
the remote possibility
that we are forced
to come out.

Not because
we want that,
of course not,
it is only stress.

There is a vital
sense in which
those preparations
cannot be wasted.

And that is
because under
any circumstances
we will need to get
ready at some point
in the near future.

Fully determined
to take advantage.

Because the course
is now set.

With
high hearts
and growing
confidence,
we will now
accelerate.

Getting ready
Be ready
Be ready

It is time we
looked not at
the risks but at
the opportunities
that are upon us.

Let us begin to
create that drive.
Let's start to liberate.
Let's feed the world.
Let's get going now
on our own timing
with all the benefits.
Let's change the rules.

That has always
been so close
to the hearts.

Yes
Let's start now.

It is more
than anything.

All this and more,
we can do now and
only now, at this
extraordinary moment.

After three years of
unfounded self-doubt
it is time to change
the record.

To recover our role
as an enterprising
outward-looking
generous in temper
engaged with the world
No one

Pluck
and
Nerve
and
Ambition

They will
not succeed
today.

We will work
flat out.

The
Work
Begins
Now

MISTAKES
WERE MADE
004

Courageous minds
of our times.

A man so admired.
His unshakeable belief
in the hidden strength
of the human spirit.

Strong
Human
Spirit

Is it ill?
The last breath

Day after night,
week after week.
Who took risks?
Most of us didn’t.

We are inspired
by empathy, bravery
and sense of duty.
I want this all
A lot

Our world
Our
Power
which will live long
Our

Expose
the fragility
around us.
A grain of sand.
How delicate
life can be.
Laid bare
The strains

The limits of
a model that
values wealth
above wellbeing
brought into
focus the fragility.
Every day
Now

It changed the
very way we behave
and communicate.
Our arms
Our faces

It showed us
fragile values.

How quickly
it can be called
into question.

Our move
Out of this world
Out of this fragility
Out of uncertainty
Ready for change
Ready to move on
This is the moment
The moment to lead
the way from this
fragility towards
a new vitality.

This is what I want.

I say this because
in the last months
we have rediscovered
the value of what we
have sacrificed.
Our personal liberty

As we shared,
we turned fear
and division into
confidence.
We showed what
is possible when
we trust each other.
Trust

With all of that we
choose to not only
repair and recover
for the here and now
but for tomorrow.

This is
This is our
opportunity to
make change
happen by design,
not by disaster.

To emerge
stronger for the
tomorrow
not just for the
yesterday.

We have
everything we need
to make this happen.

We have
shaken off the old
excuses and home
comforts that have
always held us back.

We have the vision.
We have
We have

Time to work
this morning but
I want to touch.
Focus

It is a period of
profound anxiety.
The future

Simply just getting
through until the end
of the month.

The uncertainty that
goes with it, is not over.

The recovery, in its
early stage.

Our priority
is to pull each other
through this.
To be
And to do
just that.

All human against life.
Illness
Ill-fortune
It helps us better
absorb shocks.
That enduring
promise of today.

Allow me to explain
why this is important.

No signs of running
out of steam.
Intensity can
spiral out of control.
Handle this with
extreme care.
Miracles
worked best.

Together we were home.
We stopped that.
We

Our
We
This

For me, it is crystal
clear we need a
stronger start.

Making this a
reality, we must
now draw our future.
This is why I had
proposed.

Fight for more.
Strengthen our
preparedness.

Propose
Empower
Control
Build
Support
our need.
Address
dependencies.

It is clearer than ever,
we must discuss the
question of competences.
I think this is urgent.
The Future
Because
85 we need to learn.
This is why

I will show that
this is exactly
what we have done
when it comes to
external shocks.

I knew from my experience
that these work.
They are the motor and
will be the engine.

This is why
I want this house
in record time.

Far
Elsewhere
Large

This speed of purpose
means that soon,
almost SURE, it will
give peace of mind,
income to put food
on the table or to
pay the rent.
It will help, right?
This is real action.

It reflects the fact

that the truth is too
no longer the dignity
of the entrepreneur.
Decent
Fair
Single
This is why

minimum a
must have
minimum
agreements or
minimum
respect
minimum fairness
value them
minimum

It is time.
Promise that.

Unprecedented
Unprecedented
Response needed
immediately.
Escape our history.

We flexibilised
our rules.
More
And
And
And

Took
decisive
action.

Revamped
in record time.
In record time.

This is
working with
maximum speed.

For the first time, for
exceptional times.
Put in place its
own tools.

This is
a remarkable
moment.

This is
an achievement
that we should
take pride in.

Now is the time
to hold our course.

We have
We can expect to
start moving again.
Drop the uncertainty.
This is definitely not
the time to withdraw.

A delicate balance
between support and
longer-term confidence
never been stronger.
Now use this opportunity
to make.

Our deep and
essential need.
Pre-requisite

The enduring promise
is the promise of

opportunity we may
have forgotten or
taken for granted.

We were single.
Single
All about opportunity.
For us

Cherish our safe haven
in times of trouble.
We rely on it every day
to make our lives easier.
It is critical for
recovering our strength.
Let's give it a boost.
Tear down the barriers.
Cut red tape.
Step up
Restore
in full and as
fast as possible.

The linchpin of
this is free will.
Our new strategy
for the future.
Strong
Powered
Stable
Our new strategy
Transition

The last six months
have only accelerated
that transformation,
fundamentally changing.
This is why we will
adapt our pace.
All of this

But as we pull through
together we propel
ourselves forwards.
Tomorrow there is
more urgent need.

Acceleration
It comes
Fragile
Hotter
Us
Due to collapse
Burning
We come

We longed for our
physical wellbeing.

We know change is
needed and we also
know it is possible.
Our transformation.
The heart is our mission.
We will get there.

We need to go faster
and do things better.
We
In-depth
See how fast
we could go.
Do it in a
responsible way.

We held consultation.
On this basis I recognise
that this is too much for
some and not enough
for others.

Our
Our
This
They want it too.
Just yesterday
Me
Our
This
Our obligations

If others follow I am
fully aware that many
are far away from that,
but for us, we can do it.

We have already shown
we can do it.

More
The difference
is we now have
more.
More and
More
We are
We have
More
Pushing for change.
We have
More
That what is good.
Good
Good

for us.
We have
Promise
This transformation
Our

We have a bigger
change to make.
We have it all.
Now it's our
responsibility to
make it happen.
Our energy

To get there we
must start now.
By next summer

we will make it
“fit for 55”.

Energy
Energy
Energy
Much more
It is about making.
It is about building.
Energy
We need to change
how we live and eat.
Heat

Tackle everything.

It is a real difference.
I will ensure the
next level.

We are
We are reliable.

Today we will
set a target.
Allow me to explain
how this could work.
It will

The potential

I want power
and new life.

Live and work
Our
Our need
We know that.

I want a renovation.
This is not just
a new project.
Own look and feel.
We need to give our
change its own
distinct aesthetic.
To match style
with Bauhaus.
A co-creation space.

This
That energy
Quality of life
This can only be
achieved if we do
it together.
I insist

Don't just bring
us out of the crisis.
Help us propel
forward.

Imagine for a moment
life without our family.
Cut off from
major problems.

It is in fact
not so hard
to imagine.

Learn
Work
Home
Keep running
Deliver

We saw years' worth
of transformation in the
space of a few weeks.

We are reaching the
limits of the things
we can do.

And this great
acceleration
is just beginning.
We must make this.

We need a common
plan with clearly
defined goals.
Follow clear principles.
Lead the way or follow
the way of others.

This is why we
must move fast.

There are three areas
on which I believe
we need to focus.

First
On others
And here the good
news is that we have.
We have

But the race is
not yet won.

The opportunities
that come with it.
We have the opportunity
to draw on their full
potential, worth its
weight in gold.

When it comes the
reality is never used.
This is pure waste.

On the other hand,
this is why we make it.

We need the energy.
This is why we need to
focus on, in particular,
precision, more accurate
or safe.

Open up new
worlds for us.
This world also
needs rules.

We want a set of
rules not a black box.
There must be clear
rules if something
goes wrong.

Propose next year.
Control our time.
Create a new identity.
No idea what
happens in reality.
That is why.
Propose
Trust
Do anything.

We can control
ourselves.
The point is, keep
pace with the rapid
speed of change.

We are striving
for opportunities.
Connections
Connections
Connections

This is a huge opportunity
and the prerequisite for
Revitalising
Exploit potential
Attract people
Boost

A unique chance
to focus on the unique
opportunity to develop
a more coherent approach.

None of this
is an end in itself.
It is this spirit I am

pleased to develop.
Our own

Allow this

What if to move forward
and move fast, we must
let go of our hesitancies.
This is about giving
more control.

We have
everything it takes.
Bring it to life.
Desperately waiting for this.
There has never been
a better time.

We have the ideas and
the strength to succeed.
And this is why we will.

Values
Strength
Ambitions

Transition to the world
we want to live in,
and that extends, well,
our fragility and
the challenges.

In the face of the

crisis choose to
retreat into isolation.
Actively destabilise
the system.
Reach out

Our self-serving
propaganda.
It is not
It is

Seriously
Answer the call
when it matters.

Us
Us

Wherever we live.
Whatever we have.
Most promising
The beginning
No
No
Just the rush
Be the first
to get one.
This is the moment.
Together
Whole
Unmatched
Power in action
is not enough.

100

We need to make sure.
Ensure that safe.
Afford it.
Who needs it at risk.
We are firm believers
in the strength of bodies.
Strong
We can find
long-term solutions.
Strong
Better
Strong
Fair

The truth is also that
the need has never

been so urgent.
Grown into a creeping
paralysis.
Either pulling out
or taking them hostage
for their own interests.
Neither road will
lead us anywhere.

Yes, we want change.
But change by design
not by destruction.
And this is why
I want to stop.

101 Without any doubt
there is a clear need.
Take clear positions
and quick actions.

The relationship is
simultaneously one
of the most important
and one of the most
challenging we have.
From the outset.
Partner
Competitor
Rival

We have interests
in common.

Willing to engage.
Live up to commitments.
There is still hard work.
Fair

We continue to have an
unbalanced partnership.
There is no doubt.

We believe the individual
is not without issues.
Think for example
of criticism.
Not accepted.

So we must always
call out abuses whenever
and wherever they occur.
But what holds us back?
Why are even simple
statements watered
down or held hostage
for other motives?

I say be courageous.
Finally move on.
Take a clear and
swift position.
I want to say it
loud and clear.
We have immense
courage.

Fearless
Free
Fair

The brutal response
has been shameful.

Be free
Decide own future.
Not someone else's.

Advocate closer ties.
That is not a one off.
We have seen the pattern.
Meddling around.
103 This pattern is not changing.
Change will always be
important.

While we are close
together the distance
between us appears
to be growing.

Yes
Troubled
Yes
None of this
is justification.

Always count on our
mutual interest.

The past few days is
a positive step in this
direction.

This is necessary to
create the much needed
space for dialogue.
Actions
Talks

Genuine good faith is
the only path forward.
The only path.
Lasting
More assertively

Deepen and refine
partnerships with friends.
This starts with
revitalising our most
enduring of partnerships.

We might not
always agree with
recent decisions.
We will always cherish
the unbreakable bond.

So whatever may happen
later this year, we are
ready to strengthen
our partnership.

We are ready
to work together.
Together
Jointly
With like-minded partners.
For our own good.

We need new beginnings
with old friends.
Both
Both

The scenes in this
very room when we
held hands and said
goodbye spoke a
thousand words.
They showed an
affection that will
never fade.

Every day chances
do start to fade.
We are used to that.

Navigate us through.

Talks have not
progressed as we
would have wished.
That leaves us
very little time.

As ever
Be the first to know,
have the last say.

I can assure you
we will continue to
update you throughout,
just as we did.

That took three years.
We worked relentlessly on it.
Together
Our integrity
Good

The best and only way
cannot be disregarded.

This is a matter of trust
and good faith.
And that is not just
me saying it.

I
You

It would be bad.
Bad for relations.
Bad for future.

This was true then,
and it is true today.

Trust is the foundation
of any strong partnership.
Be ready to build
strong partnerships.
Closest

Indeed
The future we share.
We share the same destiny.
We will be there.

Partnership
Partners
I
I

It was a natural choice.
It was a natural choice.
It was clear because we are.
We are natural partners.

Three months later
I returned to set
our priorities.

It is a partnership
of equals, where
both sides share
responsibilities.
Be a partner.
Building the world
we want to live in.

We will continue
to believe.
Open
Fair

Not as an end in
itself but as a way.

Home
Values
Standards
More
Make a difference.
This would be one of
the biggest acts.

High ambition
Issues
Fighting
Partnerships
Like-minded partners
Anyone else
who wants to join?

We cannot take
this for granted.
Fairness
Forward
Alone or with partners.
Want to join?
Price?
Pay the price.

Motivate
While ensuring the
same principle.
No effort
No doubt
Fall short
Long-term
Come forward

Early next year I want
to be honourable.
To play vital role in
the world, create
new vitality.
To move forward.

Overcome the
differences that
have held us back.
It can be done.

The speed with which
we took decisions.
All this shows it can
be done.
So let's do it.

An issue that has
been discussed long
enough has always
been a fact.
And it will always be.

It has defined and
shaped our lives.
And this will always
be the case.

As we know, crisis
caused many deep
divisions, with some
of those scars still
healing today.
A lot has been
done since, but a
lot is still missing.

If we are ready to
make compromises,
without compromising
on our principles,
we can find that
solution next week.

New approach
is optional.
And or more,
must be.

We have to make
a clear distinction,
right?

Stay
Do not take action.

Strengthen
Deepen partnerships.

Make sure to stay,
to feel welcome.

Future
Skills
Talent

I think of dreaming.
I think of the moment.

If we think about
what we must be

able to manage
together.

A painful reminder
of the need to come
together.

Step up here and
take responsibility.
Do just that.
Plan
Improve

I want to be clear.
If we step up
then I expect to
step up too.

Challenge
Do
Rebuild the trust.
Move forward
together.

This trust is at the
very heart of our union.
The way we do things
together.

It is anchored in
our values as Walter
used to call it.

This is not
an abstract term.
It is most basic.
It allows us to be free.
It is tool for early detection
of challenges and for
finding solutions.

I want this to be
a starting point.
No backsliding.
This is why this is
non-negotiable.

The last months
have also reminded us
how fragile it can be.

We have to always
be vigilant, to care
and nurture, to defend.

Golden values
are not for sale.
These are more
important than ever.

I say that because I
think of John who sadly
passed away this year.
He used to say that conflict
was about difference.

Respect difference.
Difference is not a threat.
Difference is natural.
Difference is the essence.

Look around
Ask where is
the essence?
Humanity
Where is
the essence?
Humanity
Where is
the essence?
Humanity
Society
Belief

This is fragile.
It is hard won but
very easily lost.

So, now is
the moment to
make change.

Action
Forward
Action
Start making
that happen.

Hate hate.
Hate is hate.

No one should have
to put up with it.
Get tougher
Because fighting
will never be optional.

We will
We will
We will
I will not rest.

You can be
who you are.
Love who you want
without fear.

Because being
yourself is your
identity and no
one can ever take
it away.

I want to be
crystal clear.
Free
Free

Make sure
Support
Put forward
Strengthen
As part of this
push for mutual
relations.

Parent
Parent

This is the world
we want to live in.
Where we are.

Where we work
together to overcome
our differences,
and pull each other
through when times
are hard.

Where we build
today and want
our children to
live in tomorrow.

But while we try
to teach our children
about life, our children
are busy teaching us
what life is about.

The last year has
shown us just how
true this really is.
We could change
for better.

Beautiful
children

There is one image
that stuck in my
mind from the last
six difficult months.

An image
The eyes
of our children.
It is the image.

Two young girls
Courage

Talent
The girls
It is the lesson
behind it.

About
not allowing
obstacles stand
in your way.

About
not letting
conventions
hold you back.

About
seizing the
moment.
This is all

Life
Every day
It is all

This
This
A leap forward
Together

When we had to
find a way forward
for our future we

did not allow old
conventions to
hold us back.

When we felt fragility
around us we seized
the moment to breathe
new vitality.

We had a choice to
go alone like we have
done in the past.

We are in this
together and we
will get out of this
together.

The future
will be what we make it.
Will be what we want it
to be.

So let's stop
talking it down.
Let's
Let's
Let's

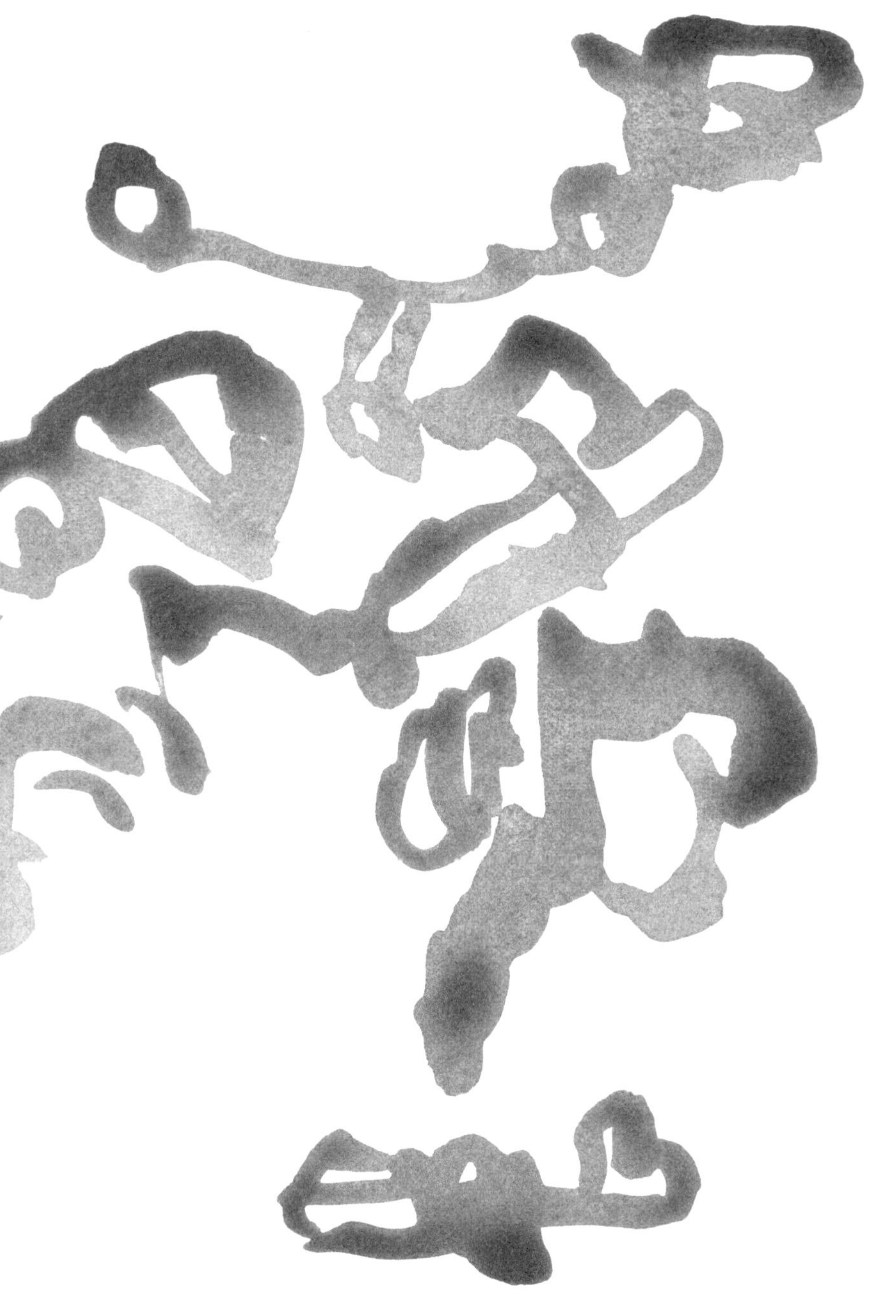

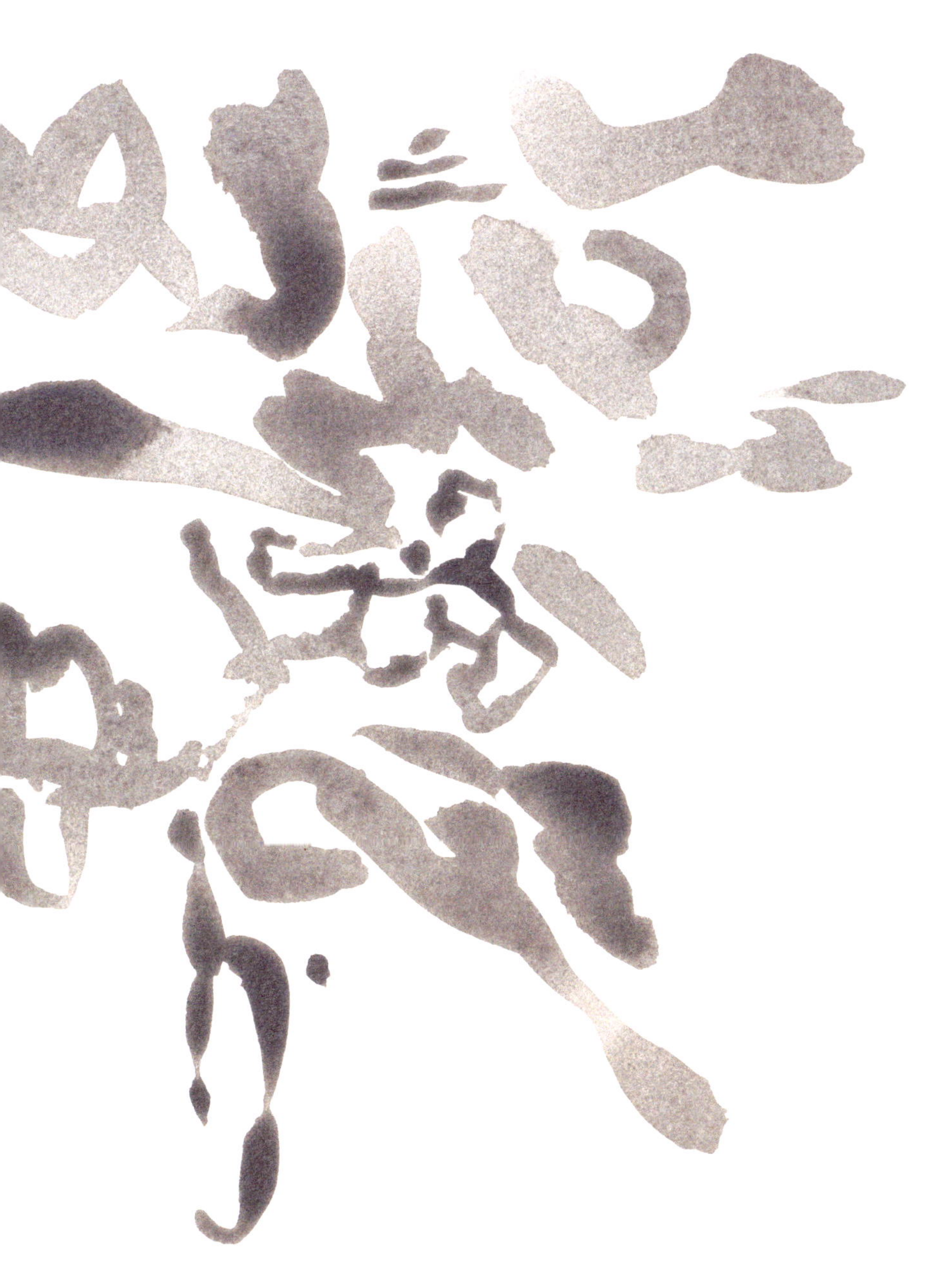

MISTAKES
WERE MADE
005

Well
This is
incredible.

When

I turned
I looked
I saw

But you don't see.
You don't want to.
We have people here
and I just want to be
recognised.

Turn please and
show what's really
happening here.

Go ahead turn,
please,
would you?

Actually,
I just really want to
see what they do.
I just want to see.
It would be really
great if we could.

The biggest problem
we have as far as
I'm concerned
Single
Biggest
Problem
Big
Big
is them.

We surprised them.
We took them
by surprise.

By the way, last night,
they didn't do a bad
job either, if you notice.

I'm honest.
I
just, again,
I want to thank you.
It's just great to be
committed to honesty
and integrity.

We will never give up.
We will never concede.
It doesn't happen.
You don't concede.

Enough
We will not take it
anymore and that's
what this is all about.

I will lay out just
some of the evidence
proving that we won.
We won it.
This was not close.

I say sometimes,
jokingly, but there's
no joke about it.
I won
I won much bigger.
The most.

They know that
we were going to
do well and we
were going to win.

I was told there was
no chance of losing.
Well
We didn't.

They say we lost.
We didn’t lose.

By the way
Does anybody believe that?
Does anybody believe that?

It’s a disgrace.
There’s never been
anything like that.

You could take,
just take a look.
What we’ve
been through.

It’s a disgrace.
It’s a disgrace.

Even when you look
at last night.
They’re all running
around like chickens
with their heads cut off.
Nobody knows what
the hell is going on.
There’s never been
anything like this.

We will not let them.
We’re not going
to let it happen.

Not going to
let it happen.

I'd love to thank you.
Great
You're
great.

But I'd love it if they
could be allowed
to come with us.
Is that possible?
Can you just let
them come, please?

171 Rudy
He's got guts.
You know what?
He's got guts.
He's got guts.
He fights.
He fights.
I'll tell you.

Fantastic
Tough
Most brilliant

He looked at
this and he said
'What an absolute
disgrace'.

He looked at
Mike, and I hope
Mike is going to do
the right thing.

I hope so.
I hope so.

Because if Mike does
the right thing we win.
All he has to do, he
has the absolute right
to do it.

We're supposed to

protect.
Support
Support and
protect.

They were given
false information.
Now they want it back.

Send it back and
we become the
happiest people.

I said
'Mike, that doesn't
take courage.
What takes courage

is to do nothing.
That takes courage'.

And then we're stuck.
We're just not going
to let that happen.

I want to thank
you for the
extraordinary love.
That's what it is.
There's never been
like this
ever
ever

Extraordinary love.
Amazing
Amazing you

By the way this goes
all the way back.
Do you believe this?
Look at this.

Unfortunately
I can't stand that.
But you look at that.
Look

That is the most
amazing sight.

You get to see it.
Amazing
Amazing

Don't worry.
We will not.
We will not
cancel culture.

They wanted to get
somebody else in there.
I don't think that's
going to happen.

It
damn
well
better
not.

Although,
if this happens,
it could happen.
You'll see some really
bad things happen.

Knock out by the way.
They've been down then
hurt.
Hurt
and everything
stopped.

Did you notice that?
It stopped.
It all stopped.

They could use
Rudy.
Rudy,
they could use
you a little.
Younger version of
Rudy.
Is that okay,
Rudy?

We're together for
one very very basic
and simple reason,
to save our evening.

And of course this
thing goes on so long.

Still, we still have no idea.
Totally lost control.

But when you see this
and when you see what's
happening, we'll never
let it happen again.

I said
'That's good,

but what about
eight weeks ago?'

I said
'I'm not interested right now.
Do me a favour, go back
eight weeks.
I want to go back
eight weeks.
Let's go back
eight weeks.'

We want to go back.
And we want to get this right.
We're not going away.

That's what.
Great

They're out there.
Fighting
Fighting
It's incredible.

I helped them.
I helped them.
I helped Mitch,
let's say.
I won't bore
you with it.

And then all of a
sudden you have

something like this.
It’s like
’Gee, maybe
sometime later.’

No, it’s amazing.
They’re pathetic and
that’s what happens.
This happened.
Hell

Just remember this.
You’re stronger.
You’re smarter.
You’ve got more going
than anybody.
You’re real.
And that’s it.

I really believe it.

I think I’m weak.
Great but weak.
Weakened

Did you see the other
day where Joe said
’I want to get rid of…’
What’s that all about
get rid of…?
How do you say
’I want to get rid of…’?

Even if you’re going
to do it don’t talk
about it.

Unbelievable what
we have to go through.

You have to fight.
Fight
Fight

I can already tell
you frankly.

But this year,
using the pretext
and the scam,
the most brazen
and outrageous theft,
there’s never been
anything like this.
It’s a pure theft
everybody knows it.

Late in the evening
or early in the morning
Boom
these explosions
and bullshit, and
all of a sudden
all of a sudden
it started to happen.

I wonder if he
enjoyed last night.

Well
I'd like to look
at the facts.

Now
I don't know.
Maybe it was okay.
Maybe that's
what happened.

Look
We've never seen
anything like it.

They talk about our,
you know, us now.

It's become the
biggest problem.

We have to do
what we caught
them doing.

Like, with his hands
tied behind his back.

We want to be so nice.
We want to be so respectful.

We're going to have
to fight much harder.
Because you're to confront
this egregious assault.

After this we're going.
And I'll be there with you.

We're going to walk.
We're going to walk
down I think.

And we're going to
cheer on women.

We're probably not
going to be cheering
so much for them,
because you have to
show strength, and
you have to be strong.

Come
Do the right thing.

Only I know that.
Everyone here will
soon see.

Stand strong.
Whether or not
stand strong.

For a long time,
far longer than this,
I thought it would
be easy.

We created.
We rebuilt.

Whether it's
four years
eight years
or more.
20 years

Now we're down to two.
I want to get it down to one.
But we're down to two.

We created.
Look at what we did.
So we create.

Which by and of
itself is a major
achievement.

And with us it's
one of so many
different things.

Right
Right

We did things
that nobody ever
thought possible.

We took care
every night.
We got that done.
We got it.

Now you don't
have to wait for
four weeks
six weeks
eight weeks
four months.

You go
You get
You have

We've not only made
life wonderful, we've
saved tremendous
amounts of money.
We've saved a lot
of money, right?

And if we see
somebody steal,
rob, do things badly
we say, get out
of here.

Before
you couldn't do that.
You couldn't do that
before.

So we've taken
care of things.

We've done things
like nobody's ever
thought possible.

And that's part of
the reason that many
people don't like us.
183 Because we've done
too much.

But we've done
it quickly.

And we were going
to sit home and watch.
It was going to be great.

And now we're out
here fighting.

I said to somebody
I was going to take
a few days and relax.
Ten o'clock, it was over.

But I was going to
take a few days.

And I can say this.
I believe, I knew
what happened,
they know what
happened.
They’re saying
Wow
Wow
Look
We were going
to be close.

To be close
To be close
To be close
We
We
We

Very important.

Right there
Right there
I’m going to be
watching.

We’re going to see
whether or not we have,
whether or not we should,

be ashamed,
throughout eternity,
ashamed.

And you know what?

If they do the wrong
thing we should never
ever forget that they did.
Never forget.
We should never
ever forget.

And by the way it's
much more important
today than it was
24 hours ago.

Because I spoke to
David, what a great
person, and Kelly
two great people.
It was a setup.

And I said
'We have no back
line anymore.'

The only back line,
the only line of demarcation,
the only line that we have
is this

I
want
the
house.

They're over there
working like you've
never seen before.
Studying
Talking
actually studying.

Because they
know we have
the right to that.

Illegally they
gave these things.
Because what did
they know?

And then when
they found out
a few weeks later,
again, it took them
four years.

And the only
unhappy person,
single most
unhappy,
is Hillary.

Because she said
'Why didn't you do this
for me four years ago?
Why didn't you do this
for me four years ago?
Change!
You could have changed!'

She's not too happy.
You don't see her anymore.
What happened?
Where is Hillary?
Where is she?

But I want to thank

all those women.

I also want
to thank
Kelly.

Kelly
I'll tell you she's
been so great.
She works so hard.

Kelly
David
they fought.
They should never
have been allowed to.
I was telling them stuff.

I actually think though
it takes, again, more
courage not to step up.

And I think those
people are going to
find that out.

You better
start looking.

We don't want to
give 2,000 to people.
We want to give them
600.

Oh great
How does that play?
Pretty good?
But how does it play?

These people we
destroyed them.
Totally
destroyed them.

We want to give
them 600 and they
just wouldn't change.

I said
'Give them 2,000.

We'll pay it back.
We'll pay it back fast.'

Give them a
couple of bucks.
Let them live.
Give them
a couple of bucks.

And some of the people
here disagree with me
on that.

But I just say
Look
you got to
let people live.

And how does
that play though?

Okay
Number one
it's the right
thing to do.

But how does
that play?

I think it's just
pure cheating.
But you can't do that.

You got to use your
head, as you know.

Outrageous lie
Widespread fraud

You ever see
these people?
'While there is no
evidence of fraud...'
Oh
really?

Well
I'm going to
read you pages.

I hope you don't get
bored listening to it.
Promise?
Don't get bored
listening to it, please.
Yeah
Don't get bored.
Don't get angry at me
because you're going to
get bored because
it's so much.

Corrupt
Fake
Ruined

But it used to be
that they'd argue
with me.

I'd fight, they'd fight.
I'd fight, they'd fight.
Boop-boop

You'd believe me,
you'd believe them.
Somebody comes
out you know.

They had their
point of view.

I had my
point of view.
But you'd have
an argument.

Now what they
do is go silent.
It's called
suppression.
And that's
what happens.
That's what they do.
They suppress.

You don't fight
with them anymore
unless it's bad.

They have a little bad
story about me, they'll
make it 10 times worse
and it's major.

But they don't
talk about him.
What happened?
They don't talk
about him.

Now watch all the
sets will go off.

Well

They can't do that
because they are
too good.

Now where is money?
How does that happen?
I'd ask you that question.
How does that happen?

Can you imagine
if I said that?
If I said that it would
be a whole different
ball game.

And how come the wife
gets hundreds of

thousands of dollars
even though he has no
millions of dollars.
How come they leave
billions of dollars to
manage?

'Have you managed
money before?'
'No, I haven't.'
'Oh, that's good.
Here's about three billion.'

No
They don't talk
about that.
No
They've gone silent.
They've gone dead.

I now realise how
good it was if you go
back 10 years.
I realised how good.

Even though I didn't
necessarily love him,
I realised how good it was.
Like a cleansing motion.

But we don't have
that anymore.

And you have to be
very careful with that.

And they've lost
all credibility.

We will not be intimidated
into accepting the hoaxes
and the lies that we've been
forced to believe over the
past several weeks.
Fake

Last night was a little bit
better because of the fact

that we had a lot of eyes
watching but they cheated
like hell anyway.

I didn't know this guy.
He said
'A friend of mine,
what's his name.'
And you know the rest.

He was
I don't know.
He was
he was doing poorly.

And
then

Stacey
Stacey
a friend of mine.
Believe it or not
she used to like me.
I was one of five.
Stacey

Brian
he weighs 130 pounds.
He said he played
offensive line in football.
I'm still trying to
figure that out.

He said that
the other night
'I was an offensive lineman.'
I'm saying
'Rcally?
That must've been
a really small team.'

But I look at that
and I look at what's
happened and he turned
out to be a disaster.

This stuff happens.

Look
I'm not happy Love.

I picked three people.
I fought like hell for them.
They all said
Cut him loose
Cut him loose
Cut him loose

I said
'No, I can't do that.
It's unfair to him.
And it's unfair
to the family.
He didn't do
anything wrong.
They're made-up stories.'

They were all
made-up stories.
He didn't do
anything wrong.
Cut him loose
I said
'No, I won't do that.'

And you know what?
They couldn't give a damn.
They couldn't give a damn, right?

But it almost
seems that they're
all going to hurt.
Hurt
Hurt

Control
I control them.
They’re puppets.
Bill
He’ll do anything
for me.

And I said
‘It really is genius’
because what they
do is that all of a
sudden Bill changed.

If you hadn’t
noticed I like Bill

but he changed.

He didn’t want to
be against me.
You know why?

Because the story is
I haven’t spoken to
any of them
any of them.

But the story is
they’re my puppet, right?
They’re puppets.

They can get out
of that because they

hate that social circus.
They do.

So I want to
congratulate them.

In fact, probably,
I'd do it the same way.
I hate to say it.

We got to get them out.
Today
For the sake of
our children.

All
changes
changes
And I think when
I say that.

So just in a nutshell,
you change.
Nobody can do it
only you.
You

'We're not going
to do that' they say.
And they go and
make the changes
themselves.

They do it anyway.
You can't do that.
So think of what
they did.

No longer
'Oh, that's okay!
by the way.'

They say
'We don't want it.'
You know why
they don't want it?
Because they
want to cheat.
That's the only
reason.

Who would even
think of that?
We don't want to.

Now think of this.
You had more
than you had.

Where did they
come from?
You know where
they came from?
Somebody's
imagination.

You had more
than you had.
And it's actually
much greater
than that.
Think of that.

That bothers
me even more.
It's incredible.

And by the way
I lost a little bit.
More than they
received.

200

In other words
what they did is
they moved back
that day.

They got back
before they were
ever out.

In other words
back before you.
They were
supposedly out.

In other words
you got back before

which is logically
and logistically
impossible.

Think of that one.
You got back.
Oh they've already
been back before.

They requested
a single giant batch,
not legal.
Illegal

You're not

allowed to do it.
It's against the law.
Yet, nobody knows
where it came from.
It remains totally
unexplained.

They said
'Well, we can't
figure that.
It appeared
from nowhere.'
Right

By the way, they
didn't know because
it was so quick.

They had all this stuff.
It's all come to light.
Doesn't happen
that fast.

The only way that can
happen is if Mike agrees.
Mike has to agree to
want it back.

Let's say you
don't do it.

Somebody says
well, we have to.

And you are because
you're protecting.
You're protecting
so you are.

But think of
what happens.

Let's say they're
stiffs and they're
stupid people.
And they say
'Well, we really
have no choice.'
Even though they
want to see.

They already have,
and as I said
it wasn't that.

You have all of the
things that we're
talking about.
But think of this.

If you don't do that,
that means you will
have lost all of these,
or you will have to put
it another way.

203 A bunch of stupid
people who lost all
of these things.

You will have.
That's what
you'll have.
And we can't let
that happen.

These are the facts
that you won't hear.

They don't want to
talk about it.
They don't want to
talk about it.

In fact
I started talking
about that.

I guarantee you
these are the things
you don't hear about.
You don't hear what
you just heard.
You don't hear it.

People want to deceive
you and demoralise you
and control you.
Just like that.

We're going to lose.
Well
We won.

They don't have
it that way because
they lose just by a
little sliver.

But they had me
the day before.

I called up.
I said
'What is that?'
'I think you're going to win.'

I said
'But why do they make it?
Because—hey, I'm not going
to waste my time.'

Love
Despite that you'll
see a lot.
It's very interesting.

If you're down let's go
and have dinner, and
let's watch television,
darling.

And just like you,
every time, even if it's
totally correct,
totally correct.
I get a flag.
I get a flag.

It's very hard to come
on to my account.
It's very hard to
get out a message.
They don't let the
message get out nearly
like they should.

But I've had
many people say

'I can't get on
your Twitter.'

I don't care
about Twitter.
Twitter is bad news.
They're all bad news.

But you know what?

I guess they call it
shadow ban.
Shadow ban
They shadow ban
you for some reason.

They don't want to put
it in there.
And they don't realise
that that's going to be
the end.

But it's never going
to be the end of us.
Never

Let them get out.
Let the weak ones get out.
This is a time for strength.

They also want children.
They want children.

It’s all part of the
standing up and saying
’No. I did nothing.’
You have
Incredible

But we didn’t do anything.
This just happened.

Two months ago
we had a massive
come down.

I said
‘What are they there for.’
They’re for you.’
We have nothing to
do with it.

And we got to
remember, in a year
from now, you’re going
to start working.

We got to get
rid of the weak
ones that aren’t
any good, Liz.
We got to get
rid of them.
We got to get
rid of them.

She never wants a
soldier brought home.
I've brought a lot
of soldiers home.
I don't know.
Some like it.
Nobody even knows.
Nobody knows.

They're great.
Their arms
Their legs
Their face
I brought
them home.

Remember I used
to say in the old days
'Don't go!'
So stupid
So stupid
And what
did we do?

We get nothing.
We never get.
We did good.
We got rid of plenty
of different things
that everybody knows.
People said it
couldn't be done.

And it was
all made
all made

This one thing
alone is much more
than we would need.
But there are
many things.

They pick them up
and they disappear
for two days.
They disappeared.

Nobody even knew
where the hell it was.
So they had no
meaning.

You know what
that is, right?
Complete defiance.

Don’t do it.
They’re the ones.
They came.

Each one of these
things we love.

I can’t believe this.

He loves conversations.
I thought it was a great
conversation personally.

People
love conversation
because it says what's
going on.

And now you have
it again last night.

Just take a look
at what happened.
What a mess.

Stacey
took them to lunch.
No clue what the hell
was happening.
Unless he did have a clue.
That's interesting.
Maybe

But we've been trying.
They won't let us do it.
The only reason they
won't, is because we'll
find things.

Why wouldn't they let us?
They won't do it.

They go to where
you would live.
I said
'That's not
the problem.
The problem is
Stacey.'

She did a good job.
I congratulate her.
But it was done
in such a way that
we can't let this stuff
happen.

We won't.
It happens.
As a result
Rejection

In other words in a
year, more than ever
before and more for
the first time.
Rejection
The only way this can
be explained is that's
the only way you could
explain it.

By the way
talking about Georgia

Rejected
Rejected
Over
Over
That's all.
We're not going
to forget it.

There's only one
reason, possibly.

You're not allowed to
ask that question.

They're ruthless

and it's time that
somebody did
something about it.

Mike
I hope you're
going to stand up.

Good
Good

And if you're not
I'm going to be very
disappointed in you.
I will tell you right now.
I'm not hearing good
stories.

Rejected
Physically
from the room.
Under the false pretence
of a pipe burst.
Water main burst.
Everybody leave.
Which we now know
was a total lie.

Oh, that sounds fair.
That was at 1:34am.

Although he says
I’m great

I sort of maybe
have to change.

He said the other day.
Yes, I disagree.
But he’s been great.

Oh
good
Thank you very much.
Him and others out,
please.

Well
now I just reached
a record low.
Rejected

Without
Over
Names and dates
More names and dates
People
Individuals
Individuals
People
Far more than we need.

Individuals underage.
Individuals who moved out.
They say they moved
right back.
They move right back.

Oh
They moved out.
They moved right back.
Okay

They miss
Georgia much.

I do
I love Georgia
Despite all of this.
Georgia
Each and every
one of us
Georgia
Big
Beautiful

Make no mistake
You
Me
Single
Single

But we haven’t yet.
You see,
you have?
You have?

They were used.
You were hurt so badly
by what took place.

Names and dates
Individuals
who had no address
and probably
didn’t live there.

Any of these things
would have taken care
of the situation.
We would have.
Any of these things
would have taken care
of the situation.
Every one of these.

Individuals
Names and dates

People who were.
That’s a great one.
Nobody knows where
they came from.

Three or four or five.
Think of that.
She witnessed them.
They came in.
They wouldn’t talk.

She also was told after
that four witnesses
have testified.

216 At 6:31am
in the early morning
hours suddenly,
it was necessary.

You know what’s
interesting?
The ones that
mattered.

In addition, there is
the highly troubling
matter of
Georgia.

Highly respected
Georgia.

It's wrong.
Think of it.
You go in and then
they tell people.
They make up
whatever they want.
Nobody's ever
even heard.

They say
'Well, we don't
think he wants to.'
Error
Error

217 There is
clear evidence
that Georgia
was reported
to have time.

Simultaneously
minutes later,
just minutes.
Going down
Going up

That was very quick.
A favour

So I mean I could go
on and on about this.

I don't want to do it to
you because I love you.
I could just go on forever
I can tell you this.

So when you hear, when
you hear wrongdoing, this
is the most fraudulent
thing anybody's
This is
This is

Because that's no good.
Do you ever see there
is no assertion?

I could go on for
another hour.
There's never been
anything like it.
Think about it.
More
More
More

But you don't have to.
I think that's almost better,
if you think, right?

More than they had.
It's a disgrace.
Is there any effort made?

Get tougher.
You're not going to
if you don't get
tougher.

They want to
play so straight.
They want to
play so, Sir, yes.

Well
I say
Yes
It says you have to.
And you have to.

And you can't.

Fraud breaks up
everything, doesn't it?

When you catch
somebody in a fraud
you're allowed to go
by very different rules.

So I hope Mike has
the courage to do
what he has to do.

I hope he doesn't listen
to the stupid people
that he's listening to.

It is widely
understood that
people have
moved out.

Individuals
who oppose every
effort to clean up.
They don’t want
to clean up.
They are loaded.

And how many
people here know
other people?

Three
Four
Five
Six
One
Seven

And then they say
you didn’t quite make it.
We won.
We won this.
They said
‘It’s not to challenge.’

You know
I mean

no matter where
you go nobody would
think this.

In fact, it’s so egregious,
it’s so bad that a lot
of people don’t even
believe it.
It’s so crazy that people
don’t even believe it.
It can’t be true so
they don’t believe it.

This is not just
a domestic matter.

You better do it
before we have left.

Today is not the end.
It’s just the beginning.

With your help nobody
even challenges that.
I say that over and over
and I never get challenged.
And they challenge
almost everything.

Our fight against others
is just getting started.
This is the greatest.
Never been like that.

You look back.
It’s hard to believe.

We must ensure that
such outrageous fraud
never happens again,
can never be allowed
to happen again.

We’re going forward.
We’ll take care of
going forward.
We got to take care
of going back.

Don’t let them talk.
Okay
Well
We promise.

I said
‘I’m not interested
right now.
I’m interested
in right there.’
With your help finally.

You need cash?
You need to go
to a bank?
Buy alcohol?
Drive a car?

Every person
should need most
important thing.

We will
We just had
We will
Therefore
they get.

They disappear and
then all of a sudden
they show up.

We will clean up.
Ensure honest manner.

We will restore the vital
tradition when they
make their choice.

We will finally hold
big courage and guts.

All of these are going
to abuse their power
and it has to be stopped.

Get a lot tougher.
They should be.
They're together.
We will clean up.

We have done
a big job on it.

You think it’s easy?
It’s dirty
It’s dirty

You have a lot
of bad people
out there.

Despite everything
we’ve been through.
Looking out and seeing
this, I think, is our
all-time record.

Here today
I have never been
more confident
in our future.

Well
I have to say
we have to be a
little bit careful.

That’s a nice
statement but
we have to be a
little careful with
that statement.

If we allow this to
take over our way.

We are the greatest
and we are headed
in the right direction.
You know
Flow
Flow

We did a great job.
Remember?
They said it could
never be done.
The largest
we've ever had.

It's had a tremendous
impact and we got rid of
all of the stuff that we
had to live with.

But now they want
to come in again.
Can't let it happen.

We have truth
on our side.
We have a deep
and enduring love
in our hearts.
Love

We have overwhelming
pride, and we have it
deep in our souls.

Together we
are determined.

Our
brightest days
are before us.

Our
greatest
achievements
still wait.

Our
great
achievements.

Nobody
until I came along
had any idea.

And again
most people
would stand there
and say
'I want to thank
you very much,'
and they go off
to some other life.

But I said
'Something's wrong here.
Something's really wrong.
Can't have happened.'

And we fight.
We fight like hell.

And if you don't
fight like hell, you're
not going to have
exciting adventures.

Boldest
endeavours

For our children
Beloved
I say this.

Despite all
that's happened,
the best is yet
to come.

So we're going to.
We're going to love.
And we're going
to try and give.

We're going
to try and help.

We're going
to try and give
them the kind of
pride and boldness
that they need.

I want to
thank you
for being
incredible.

MISTAKES
WERE MADE
006

This day
A day of hope.
Of renewal
And resolve
Tested anew.

Risen to the
challenge.

We celebrate
the triumph.

The cause,
we have learned,
is precious.
Fragile

And at this hour
has prevailed.

So now this violence
sought to shake
this very foundation.

We come together.
Indivisible

We look ahead
restless
bold
optimistic

We know we can be
and we must be.

I thank them from the
bottom of my heart.
You know

The resilience
and the strength.

As does Carter, who
I spoke to last night.

The story depends
not on one of us,
not on some of us,
but on us who seek
a more perfect union.

This is great
and we are good.
Through storm
and strife we have
come so far.

But we still have
far to go.

We will press forward
with speed and urgency
for we have much to
do this winter.
Much to repair
Much to restore
Much to heal
Much to build
Much to gain

Few periods have been
more challenging or
difficult than the one
we’re in now.

It’s taken one year.
Millions have been lost.
Hundreds of thousands.

A cry moves us.
Dream no longer.
Cry for itself.
A cry that can’t be
any more desperate
or any more clear.

Rise
Confront
Defeat

To overcome these
challenges, to restore
the soul and to secure
the future, requires
more than words.

It requires that most
elusive of things
Unity
Unity

In January
On New Year's Day,
he said
'My whole soul is in it.'

'My whole soul is in it.'

Today
On this January day,
my whole soul is in this.
Together
Uniting
Uniting

Join me in this.
Fight the common
foes we face.

Anger
Resentment
Hatred
Violence

Joblessness
Hopelessness

We can do
great things.
Important things.
We can right
wrongs.
We can work
in good jobs.
Our children
in safe schools.
We can
We work and care.
We can

We can
Once again
Force good

I know speaking of
unity can sound like
a foolish fantasy.
I know the forces that
divide us are deep
and they are real.
But I also know
they are not new.

A constant struggle
between the ideal
that we are and the
harsh ugly reality.

That fear
Torn apart
Never assured
Depression
Struggle
Sacrifice
Setbacks
have always
prevailed.

In each of these
moments enough
came together to
carry us forward.

And we can do so now.

The way of unity.
We can see each other.
We can treat each
other with dignity
and respect.
We can join forces.

Stop the shouting.
Lower the temperature.
There is only bitterness
and fury.

No progress.
Only exhausting outrage.
Only chaos.

This is our moment
of crisis and challenge,
and we must meet
this moment.

If we do that,
I guarantee you,
we will not fail.

We have
never
ever
ever
failed when
we have acted
together.

And so today,
at this time
and in this place,
let us start afresh.
Us

Let us listen
to one another.
Hear one another.
See one another.
Show respect
to one another.

Not be a raging fire
destroying everything.

Every disagreement
doesn't have to be
a cause for total war.

We must
We have
to be different
than this.
To be better
than this.
Better
than this.

Just look around.
Here we stand
in the balance.
We endured and
we prevailed.

Here we stand.
Here we stand, right?
Today don't tell me
things can't change.
Here we stand.
Full of devotion.
In peace
Here we stand.
Just days after violence.
Silence

That did not happen.
It will never happen.

Not today
Not tomorrow
Not ever

I am humbled by
the faith you have
placed in us.

All those who did
not support us.
Hear
As we move forward.

Take a measure of
me and my heart and
237 if you still disagree
so be it.

That’s our greatest
strength.

Hear me clearly.

Disagreement must
not lead to disunion.
I pledge this to you.
I will fight hard for love.

What are the
common objects we
love that define us?
I think I know.

Dignity
Respect
and yes
the truth

Recent weeks
and months have
taught us a
painful lesson.

There is truth
and there are lies.
Lies

Defend the truth

and defeat the lies.

I view the future with
fear and trepidation.

I worry about jobs
about what comes next.
Get it?

But the answer is
not to turn inward,
to retreat, distrusting
those who don't like
you or worship you
or don't get their
news from the same
sources you do.

End this

We can do this
if we open our souls
instead of hardening
our hearts.

Show a little
tolerance
and humility.

Stand in the other
person’s shoes just
for a moment.

Because here is
the thing about life.

There is no
accounting for
what fate will
deal you.

There are some days
when we need a hand.

There are other days
when we’re called on
to lend one.

That is how we must
be with one another.

And if we are this way
Stronger
More prosperous
More ready for the
future in the work
ahead of us.
We will need each other.

We will need
all our strength
to persevere through
this dark winter.

We are entering
what may well be the

toughest period.
We must face
this as one.
I promise you this.
We will get through
this together

Today
We have come
out stronger.

We will engage with
yesterday’s challenges
today’s and tomorrow’s.

We will
We will be strong.

We have been
through so much.
I like you
Remember

All we lost this
past year.
Those 400,000.
We know we
should be silent.

This is a time
of testing.
We face a raging
growing crisis.

Enough to challenge
us in profound ways.
All at once.
With the gravest of
responsibilities.
Now we must
step up.
Us

It is a time for
boldness, for there
is so much to do.

And this is certain.
We will be judged.
You and I
We

Will we rise
to the occasion?
Will we master
this rare and
difficult hour?
Will we meet
our obligations?

Our children
believe we must.
And I believe we will.
And when we do
we will write the
next chapter in
the story.

It’s a story that
might sound
something like a
song that means
a lot to me.

It’s called
’One for me’

’This day,
what shall
be our legacy?
What will our
children say?
Let me know
in my heart.

When my days
are through.
I gave my best
to you.’

Let us add our
own work to the
unfolding story.

If we do this,
then when our
days are through
our children and
our children’s children
will say of us, they
 gave their best.
They did.
They healed.

I give you my word.
I will always
I will
I will
I will
I will give my all.

Thinking not of
possibilities of
personal interest.
Together
We shall hope
not fear.

Of unity
Of love
Of healing
Of goodness

The story that guides us.
The story that inspires us.
The story yet to come
that we met and thrived.
Our home
That is what we
owe one another.

So, with purpose and
resolve we turn to the
tasks, devoted to one
another, and to love
with all our hearts.

MISTAKES WERE MADE 011

Es ist eine gute Tradition.
Diese Tradition.

Respektvoll im Umgang.
Orientiert an der Sache.
Immer mit dem Willen zu
gemeinsamer Gestaltung.

Das biete ich und
darum bitte ich.

Diese Ziele leiten uns.
Wir wollen eine gute Zukunft.
Gemeinsam

Ich bin gern gekommen,
weil dieser Besuch für mich
eine Art Heimkehr ist.

Hier
Am richtigen Ort.
Der Ausgleich

Zunächst aber lieber
noch nachträglich
gratulieren.

Auch für uns nicht
einfach zu bewältigen.
Immer wieder dafür

sorgen, dass alles
reibungslos funktioniert.
Sich bewährt.

Wir haben Lösungen
gefunden, die sich
eben nicht immer gleich
entwickelt haben.
Und die Grundlage
geschaffen.
Das war wichtig für
die Akzeptanz.

Vor allem aber
bringt uns das
verhältnismäßig
gut durch.

Weniger
Geringer
Trotz großer
Belastungen
standgehalten.

Das zeigt, unsere
Maßnahmen wirken.

Wir
Vor allem
Besonders
Gerade
Zum Glück

247 Wir sollten alles
daran setzen,
dass dies so bleibt.
Dass der Höhepunkt
in Sicht ist.

Das erlaubt uns
nächste Woche und
dann das Frühjahr
in den Blick zu nehmen.

Wie bisher
werden wir uns
dabei leiten lassen.
Denn wir wollen
unseren Erfolg jetzt
nicht aufs Spiel setzen.

Zugleich werden
wir wachsam und
vorbereitet sein.
Für den Fall
Eins ist klar.

Deshalb setzen wir
auch weiter alles
daran zu überzeugen.

Ich sage auch
Gemeinsam
Gemeinsam

Es geht jetzt

um den Schutz.
Schutz muss und
wird weiterhin
höchste Priorität
für uns haben.
Liebe macht
auch Sinn.

Wichtig ist mir
auch, dass wir
Lehren für die
Zukunft ziehen.

Die
vorsorgenden
krisenfesten
modernen.

Konkret werden,
zum Beispiel.

Stärken
Schaffen
Die Attraktivität
erhöhen.

Was leisten
ist mehr als
beeindruckend.

Bewährungsprobe
bestanden.
Leid verursacht.
Von
Bis
Zum

In dieser Lage
Entschlossen dabei
Massiv unterstützt

Es hat sich gezeigt,
wenn es darauf
ankommt, dann
stehen wir zusammen.

Das war ein großer
Lichtblick, deren
Folgen uns noch lange
beschäftigen werden.

Ein handfestes Zeichen
Ein starkes Bekenntnis
zum Prinzip der geteilten
Kompetenzen.

Leider werden die
Vorzüge manchmal
unterschätzt.
Abschätzig ist dann
grundsätzlich besser.
Eine Sehnsucht
wohlgemerkt.

Diese Tendenz
Es gibt sie ja,
tatsächlich.
Und das sollte uns
zu denken geben.

Tatsächlich ein
entscheidender
Grund.

Die Stärke trägt
ebenso Rechnung.

Möglichst verknüpft.
Gemeinsame Möglichkeit
passgenauer Lösungen.

Und gerade
das tut gut.

Als ein Ehemaliger
weiß ich wie
gewinnbringend
die Suche nach
Kompromissen ist.

Diese Kultur sollten
wir uns unbedingt
bewahren.
Und zwar gerade
wenn, und gerade weil
die Kompromissfindung
nicht einfacher wird.

Im Jahr 2005

sechs verschiedene
fünf
16
noch jeweils
eine allein
und
elf.

Heute
16
15 verschiedene
und
acht.

Solche Vielfalt
ist nicht einfacher.
Wir tragen besondere

Verantwortung dafür.
Jederzeit

Ziel
Die Enge

Für uns nicht
nur ein Gebot
der Vernunft.

Sie ist mir auch
ein persönliches
Herzensanliegen.

Kein starres
Gefüge, sondern
eine gewachsene,
lebendige Ordnung,
die immer wieder
austariert werden
muss.

Angepasst

Das waren wichtige
Schritte.

Die vergangenen
Jahre haben gezeigt,
dass wir vielleicht
an manchen Stellen
von einer noch

klareren Aufteilung
der Aufgaben
profitieren könnten.

Ich denke und bin
sicher, dass wir
hier vorankommen
werden.

Endlich
Gemeinsam lösen
wir das Problem
aus eigener Kraft.

Einen Neustart
253 Die Chance bekommen
Eine gute Zukunft
Wir
Gemeinsam
Bereit

Gelingen wird
dies nur im Konsens
und nur durch
eine Änderung.

Ich habe gerade
schon aufgezeigt, wie
engagiert er seinerseits
gewesen ist.
Das sollten wir
nicht ganz außer

Acht lassen, wenn
wir künftig reden.

Die Bereitschaft
werden wir auch
brauchen, um die
wohl größte
Herausforderung
zu meistern.

Vor uns liegt
nichts Geringeres
als eine zweite
Revolution.
Wir wollen, nein,

wir müssen die
meistern.

Dafür werden wir
jetzt mutig die
einzigartigen Chancen
nutzen, die wir wie
wenige andere haben.
Intensiv

Alle notwendigen
Vorhaben werden wir
in den kommenden
Jahren tätigen.
Deshalb werden
wir die richtigen
Anreize setzen.

Eines ist dafür
ganz entscheidend.
Privat

Es gibt Beispiele
oder Planung.
Das ist zu lange.

Wir müssen viel
schneller werden.
Dramatisch
beschleunigen.

Auch das wird
gelingen.

Massive Energien

Wir
können
brauchen
schaffen
wollen

Dann müssen wir
möglichst reibungsfrei
ineinandergreifen.
Wir
Gemeinsam

Dafür wünsche ich mir
die Unterstützung.

Ein weiteres Thema
liegt mir am Herzen.
Das ist das Thema
so heftig diskutiert.
Die Zukunft
und die Kinder.

Die Defizite, die
wir erlebt haben,
müssen wir abstellen.
Das gilt bei dieser
zentralen Aufgabe.

verlässlich
dauerhaft
256 zusammen

Es geht darum unsere
Kräfte zu bündeln.
Ziel
Bestmögliche zu
ermöglichen.

Das Beispiel zeigt
uns ja, wie riesengroß
das Potenzial ist.
Wie es ankommt.
Dieses Potenzial
Hand in Hand

Zusammen wachsen,
zusammenwachsen.

Gerade in seiner
doppelten Bedeutung
verweist es auf das,
was auch nach 32 Jahren
noch zu tun bleibt.

Daraus folgt, dass
wir noch deutlich
näher kommen
müssen, dass alles
überall gleich ist.

Es bedeutet
Überall ähnlich
Es bedeutet
Nirgendwo darf sich
die Wahrnehmung
breitmachen.

Das ist im Übrigen
auch eine Frage
des Respekts.
Des Respekts

Sich unter schwierigen
Bedingungen anstrengen
und etwas leisten.
Handfest

Dieser
Dieses
Auch für mich.

Den Eindruck haben,
dass die Chancen
und Belastungen
gerecht sind.

Veränderungen
Vertrauen
Vorhaben
Verantwortung
Viel darüber
gesprochen.

Jetzt kommt es
darauf an zu handeln.

Dazu zählt das.
Dazu zählt etwas zu tun.

Und in diesen Tagen
weiß jeder genau,
warum das wichtig ist.

Ein erster Schritt,
weitere werden folgen.

Dazu zählt unser
klares Ziel.

Wir haben einen
vernünftigen Weg
gesucht, der in
die Zukunft trägt.

Wir werden
Perspektiven haben.

Unterschiede
behalten wir fest
im Blick.

Darum habe ich
entschieden bei allen
Aufgaben, die wir
bewältigen müssen,
dürfen wir eines
nicht vergessen.

Unser

wichtigstes
Anliegen
ist das Gelingen.

Das ergibt sich aus
unserer
unserer
unserer
Vernetzung

Wir brauchen
unser Engagement.

Wie wichtig
das ist, das
erleben wir
gerade jetzt,

in dieser Zeit
der Sorgen.

Es ist unsere Aufgabe
dafür Sorge zu tragen,
dass wir einig sind.

Dazu gehört auch,
dass wir gleichzeitig
alle Möglichkeiten zu
Gesprächen nutzen.

Zusammen einen Ausweg
aus der seit vielen
Jahren so verfahrenen
Situation zu finden.

Gerade gestern.
Ein Gespräch
Stundenlang

Ich werde nächste
Woche fahren.

Alles dient dazu,
dass wir genau das
erreichen.

Und das ist aller
Anstrengung wert.

Zu verletzlich

Umso mehr
kommt es darauf
an zu haben.
Einen wichtigen
Schritt getan.

Aber für mich
ist klar.

Um unsere
Verletzlichkeit
dauerhaft zu
verringern, müssen
wir mutig vorangehen.

261 Unsere Lebensweise
auch künftig
selbstbestimmt
gestalten.

Darin sind wir
uns einig.

Ich denke dabei
zum Beispiel
an die Zukunft.
Ja
Direkt

Erfolgreich
sind wir immer.
Immer wieder.

Darauf baue
ich auch jetzt.

Klar ist,
Zusammenhalt
erreichen wir nur
gemeinsam.

MISTAKES
WERE MADE
009

I have just stood up
to aggression.

A hugely consequential
take on responsibility.

Vital for our belief in
enterprise and in fair play.

Grit
Courage
Determination
Time and time
again.

We now face headwinds
caused by appalling
aftermath of time.
Issues that are back.

We
We need more.
We need to
reduce the burden.
Get on in life.

I know that we
have what it takes
to tackle those
challenges.

Of course it
won't be easy.
But we can do it.
We will

Aspiration
High-paying jobs
where everyone
everywhere has
the opportunities
they deserve.

Action this day.
Action every day.
Make it happen.
We will

We can't have home
without having three
priorities.

Firstly
working again.

I have a bold plan.
To grow and cut.
To work and boost.

Growth
My mission
Working and growing.

We will get spades
in the ground.
Sure we will.
Sure

Secondly
I will deal hands-on
with the crisis.
I will take action
this week to deal
with our future.

Thirdly
I will make sure that
we will put our health
on a firm footing.
On the path to
long-term success.

We shouldn't be
daunted by the
challenges we face.
As strong as the
storm may be
I get things done.

We have talent energy
and determination.

I am confident that
together we can ride
out the storm and
become brilliant.
That I know we can be.

PS

At a time of instability,
worried about how to pay
bills, held back for too long,
I party to change energy.

Set out a vision.
Take advantage of

the freedoms.
I recognise though,
given the situation,
I cannot party.

I have spoken to him
that I party this morning.
We have agreed, in the
next week, we remain on
a path to maintain our will.

267

MISTAKES WERE MADE 010

Good
I have accepted
his invitation.

It is only right to
explain why I am
here right now.

Profound crisis
The aftermath
still lingers.

I want to
pay tribute.

She was not
wrong to want
to improve.

It is
a noble aim.

And I admired
her restlessness
to change.

But
some
mistakes
were
made.

Not borne of ill
will or bad intentions.

Quite the opposite
in fact.

But mistakes
nonetheless.

My
your
in part.

Fix them.
Immediately

I will place
confidence
at the heart.

This will mean
difficult decisions
to come.

269 You saw me doing
everything I could.
Protect
Like

There are
always limits.
More so now
than ever.

But I promise
you this.

I will bring that
same compassion
to the challenges
we face today.

I will not leave
your children with
a debt to settle that
we were too weak
to pay ourselves.
I will not

Words
But with
action

I will work day in
and day out for you.
At every level.

Trust is earned.
And I will earn yours.
I will

Be grateful for his
incredible achievements.
His warmth and
generosity of spirit.
I know he would agree.

That is not the
property of one
individual.
It belongs to us.

The heart is our.
Promise

Stronger
Better
Safer
Control
Protecting
Supporting
Embraces

I understand
how difficult this
moment is.

It cost us, after all,
the dislocation
that must be seen
successfully to
its conclusions.

I fully appreciate
how hard things are.

And I understand too
that I have work to do
to restore trust after
all that has happened.

All I can say is that
I am not daunted.
I know

I hope to live up
to demands.

But when the opportunity
comes along you cannot
question the moment,
only your willingness.

I
before you
Ready?

Our future
Your needs
Reach out

Together we can
achieve incredible
things.

We will create a
future worthy of the
sacrifices and fill
tomorrow and every
day thereafter
with hope.

MISTAKES WERE MADE develops Agata Madejska's ongoing interest into the fissures of institutional power by looking closer at the linguistic structures of contemporary politics.

The collection of poems at the core of MISTAKES WERE MADE are deconstructed speeches made by Western leaders between 2016 and 2022—pronouncements which mark the beginning or the end of a political reign.

Transformed into jittering, self-affirming monologues, here, the political content of these public announcements has been removed. Debased of rhetorical action, Madejska's editing exposes the patterns of persuasion that colour the play of contemporary political practice.

This publication not only brings together transcriptions of these ominous proclamations but positions them next to a range of abstract light-sensitive drawings.

Operating in a manner similar to courtroom sketches, these drawings are instinctive gestures made by the artist as she pays witness to the narrative flows of political rhetoric.

Loose and ephemeral, they record how the lulling voice of politics infiltrates the body, directing one's movements through as well as one's adaptations to life.

In an age of ever-increasing radicalisation and shifting narratives within mainstream discourse, MISTAKES WERE MADE asks us to look beyond the facade of our political architecture and to become more cognisant of the grains that dictate our social being.

I would like
to thank

Gareth Bell-Jones
Gisela Bullacher
Emily Butler
Mathias Clottu
Carole Courtillé
Mary Cork
Mafalda Dâmaso
Diana Fiedler
Maël Fournier-Comte
Adam Gibbons
Anna Gritz
Martin Groß
Erik Hartin
Julius Heinemann
Mary Hurrell
Dorothea Jendricke
Emma Kasyan
Judith Lehmkuhl
Peter Otto
Teofil Otto
Moa Pårup
Toby Üpson
Eva Wilson
and my family.

Special thanks
for all the support
to Belmacz and
Julia Muggenburg.

Published by
Edition Taube
München

Co-published by
Belmacz
London

Limited edition
501 copies

Designed by
PARAT.cc
Agata Madejska

Printed by
DZA
Druckerei zu Altenburg

Distributed by
Antenne Books (UK)
Twelve Books (JP)
Idea Books (World)
editiontaube.de

ISBN: 978-3-945900-96-3